Joseph and His Brothers

Genesis 37–47 for children

Written by Teresa Olive
Illustrated by Elizabeth Swisher

ARCH® Books

3558 S. Jefferson Avenue, St. Louis, MO 63118-3968
Manufactured in the United States of America

Jacob had twelve sons, but the two he loved the best
Were Benjamin and Joseph, who were younger than the
rest.
Jacob made for Joseph a special coat to wear.
His older brothers envied him; they thought it wasn't
fair.

Joseph's coat was beautiful, yet all *their* coats
were plain.
They started feeling angry. They started to complain.
Then Joseph told them something that really made
them mad:
"Listen now, my brothers, to the dream that I just had.

"All of us were bundling the grain upon the ground.
Suddenly, my bundle stood, and yours all kneeled around."
Then Joseph had another dream. He told his family,
"The sun, moon, and eleven stars were bowing down to me."

His brothers said, "You really think that we'll bow down to you?"
They hated Joseph even more—his dreams must not come true!
Later, Joseph went to find his brothers in the field.
When they saw him coming up, their hatred was revealed.

They said, "There's that dreamer walking up our way.
Let's kill and dump him in a well—his dreams will end today!"
They grabbed Joseph's fancy coat and tore it off his back.
They threw him in an empty well; he landed with a *whack!*

Then they saw the dust rise from a distant caravan.
Joseph's brother Judah said, "I've got a better plan.
Why should we kill Joseph? Let's just sell him
as a slave."
Twenty silver pieces was the price the merchants gave.

The brothers dipped his coat in blood to hide what they
had done.
They didn't want their dad to know they'd sold his
favorite son!
Jacob saw the coat and cried, "Some creature in the wild
Must have eaten Joseph!" He mourned for his lost child.

A captain down in Egypt bought young Joseph
before long.
His wife had Joseph thrown in jail, although he'd done
no wrong.
Joseph was in prison, yet God blessed him even there.
Soon the other prisoners were put in Joseph's care.

A baker and a butler in the jail with him had dreams.
God helped Joseph tell them what each dream would
really mean.
As Joseph had explained, the baker died in three
days' time.
The butler was released to serve the Pharaoh cups of
wine.

Two years later, Joseph still in prison did remain,
Until the Pharaoh had two dreams that no one could
explain.
Then the butler told the king, "I had a dream in jail.
A man there told me what it meant, down to the last
detail."

So Pharaoh sent for Joseph and said, "What do my
dreams mean?
I saw seven fat cows gobbled up by seven lean.
My second dream had seven fat and skinny heads
of grain.
The thin ones ate the chubby ones but still looked just
the same."

Joseph said to Pharaoh, "God has shown you what's
to come.
We'll have seven years with food, then seven years with
none."
Pharaoh said, "There's no one else so wise in
all my land.
Go store our grain for seven years. You're second in
command!"

As Joseph said, when seven years of plenty were
all done,
A famine came, but Joseph had saved food for everyone.
Even far-off Canaan hadn't had a drop of rain,
So Jacob sent his oldest sons to Egypt to buy grain.

They bowed down to Joseph, whom they
did not recognize.
Joseph knew who *they* were but said, "You must be
spies!"
"We are ten sons out of twelve—one's home and one
is dead.
We just came to buy some grain!" the frightened men all
said.

“To prove you’re honest, bring the youngest son when
you come back,”
Joseph said as servants put their grain into each sack.
They went home, but soon the grain was eaten up again.
So tearfully, their father sent them off with Benjamin.

When Joseph saw that they had brought his youngest brother up,
He filled their sacks but hid in one his special silver cup.
Then his servants found the cup inside the youngest's sack
And said, "This thief must be a slave to pay our master back!"

The brothers went to Joseph's house, where Judah
humbly said,
"Please, sir, let my brother go—make *me* your slave
instead!"
When Joseph heard him beg, he could not stand
it anymore.
He told his servants all to go, and then he shut the door.

He cried out, “I’m your brother! I am Joseph,
can’t you see?”
Then they recognized him and they trembled fearfully.
But Joseph said, “My brothers, please do not be afraid.
Because I’m here, our family and others have been
saved.”

Joseph had forgiven them in spite of all they'd done.
He knew that God had used it for the good of everyone.
Then Jacob and his sons all went to Egypt's land to live
With Joseph, who had shown them all God's power to forgive.

Dear Parents:

God sent Joseph's great-grandfather Abraham to the land of Canaan. There God called His people to live a life sharply separated from the surrounding nations as He began to carry out the covenant that would result in the birth, death, and resurrection of His Son. Jealousy, famine, and revenge could not defeat God's plan. Joseph became God's instrument to lead His people to Egypt and save them from starvation.

We know that in all things God works for the good of those who love Him, who have been called according to His purpose (Romans 8:28). Discuss some thoughts or events that may be troubling your child. Thank God for His promise to work for our good in every situation. And thank Him for His plan of salvation in Jesus that embraces your family and people of all times and places.

The Editor